A Christmas Posy

Also by Judith E.P. Johnson
Mountain Moods (VDL Publications, 1997)
Gatherers (VDL Publications, 1998)
Fragments (VDL Publications, 2000)
Selected Poems CD (7 RPH, 2001)
Snapshot (Regal Press, 2003)
Landmarks (Ginninderra Press, 2005)
Alone at the Window (Ginninderra Press, 2012)
Between Two Moons (Ginninderra Press, 2015)
Waking from Dreams (Ginninderra Press, 2016)
Where It Leads (Ginninderra Press, 2018)
Only the Waves (Ginninderra Press, 2019)
Briefly in Spring (Ginninderra Press, 2020)
Day Moon Fading (Ginninderra Press, 2021)
Earth from the Moon (Ginninderra Press, 2022)

Judith E.P. Johnson

A Christmas Posy

haiku & senryu

Acknowledgements

The author has had many haiku published in journals, on radio and online. All the haiku in *A Christmas Posy* are new, except for those which appeared in the author's previous books, in *Prospect* and in *Kô*.

Special thanks are due to Peter Macrow for his kindness and inspiration, to my children Karen, Debra and Craig for their encouragement and support, to Jane Williams for editing this book and to Katherine Johnson for the cover design.

A Christmas Posy: haiku & senryu
ISBN 978 1 76109 603 7
Copyright © text Judith E.P. Johnson 2023
Cover: Katherine Johnson

First published 2023 by
Ginninderra Press
PO Box 3461 Port Adelaide SA 5015
www.ginninderrapress.com.au

for Graeme
and also for my mother
who made the Christmas posy

December first
children counting
sleeps

tissue-wrapped gifts
white sky
and silver stars

yuletide
following winter customs
summer sun

airless heat
a child tinkles
the wind chime

cathedral bell
a flock of sparrows
out of the elms

soaring
into domed silence
Handel's Messiah

Santa photo
the eldest child
not smiling

Christmas heatwave
in the post
another snow scene

homemade
strung wall to wall
doll's house streamers

sleeping child
shadows fill
the empty stocking

family dinner
I light a candle
for those not there

red rose buds
and mock orange
mother's Christmas posy

kinder crafts
she brings home
a toilet roll Santa

the silly season
blowing
the budget

raffle
at the corner store
giant Christmas stocking

into the pudding
each child stirs
a silent wish

missing you
I rearrange
the ornaments again

surprise
a gift bag
on the front door

watching
at the starry window
the child asleep

bright tree lights
outside
finches in the hibiscus

still dancing
after the music
the young couple

treetop star
leaving gifts
paper-winged children

wind-up Santa
fifty years on
runs off the table

small town
in a glass bauble
sudden snowstorm

Advent
mother puts up
her childhood calendar

school play
a shepherd's crook
grandpa's walking stick

we three kings…
no wise men
three women act the part

late drive home
children count
the Christmas trees

muggy heat
along mother's path
iceberg roses

every year
the good, the bad
her Christmas letter

birch rod
Krampus
scatters the children

knitted bear
used wrapping paper
ironed

a gift card for you
a goat
for someone else

tickling my cheek
the child's
butterfly kiss

department store
designer trees
silver and gold

stained-glass window
sunlit
the Madonna and child

lights out
how limp the stocking
at the end of the bed

holy days
returning home
sacred places

behind the story
somewhere
another story

shells and seaweed
driftwood branch
a child's festive tree

fifteen cents
her old stamp collection
Santa in shorts

humid room
from the record player
sleigh bells and snow

from Santa's sack
a toy for each child
he knows by name

wattle
around the shack doorway
pudding aroma

temptingly built
in the shop window
gingerbread house

father and child
in a quiet corner
new building blocks

old stone church
a village choir sings
o little town…

flowering
in foreshore grasses
Christmas bells

playing
in cast-off gift wrap
toddler and dog

sun round
great grandmother's shortbread
from Scottish snow

bottlebrush bees
sparrows in the birdbath
noonday heat

childhood recall
true or not
it is so

roses
on the polished table
reflections of home

arcade photo
the dog
on Santa's knee

carols in the park
your candle lights the child's
and mine

fruit mince pies
at each bakery
the best

fresh from your kitchen
mother's Christmas cake
thirty years on

toys everywhere
the toddler puts my cup
on the sink

wreath
on the front door
gum leaves and wild flowers

shack fun and games
laughing
the kookaburra

waving Santa
small child holds mother's hand
tighter

primary school play
Joseph
sweeps the stable

midnight
in suburban darkness
the church all lit up

stranger down the chimney
small child asks
why not the front door?

snowstorm
the window view
spray-painted

sky star bright
valley silence
dark with dreams

dawn laughter
children and stockings
crowd the double bed

welcoming guests
tinsel
on the dog's collar

descending
on the old home
absent family

in all the fun
don't forget
the sleeping baby

oven failure
a neighbour cooks
the turkey

through it all
the cat asleep
on great-aunt's lap

waiting in ambush
children
and water pistols

Santa's sleigh
circling
painted glass globe

nativity set
moving Joseph
to cut a slice

opening presents
a granddaughter
on either side

hot evening
all through the house
a late sea breeze

after plum pudding
father retells
the cracker jokes

coming in at 6 a.m.
next-door's kids
sent home

sleight of hand
a pudding trinket
in each slice

white Christmas
memory of wine
chilling in the snow

Christmas bootee
in the bassinet
wide-eyed baby

celluloid star
so many Christmases
long forgotten

Christmas Day
grandparents on video call
snowed-in

child's card homemade
some of the glitter
on my face

dinner at grandma's
she dusts off
her Royal Albert

another helping
great uncle
says grace again

pedal car and pram
brother and sister
swap toys

guests gone
the house darkens
to one lighted room

balcony dinner
for two
just Santa and I

rocking horse
after the child
still rocking

Boxing Day
still feasting
new books

next year's calendar
all those empty spaces
to live

www.ingramcontent.com/pod-product-compliance
Lightning Source LLC
Chambersburg PA
CBHW071034080526
44587CB00015B/2606